The Puzzle of Books

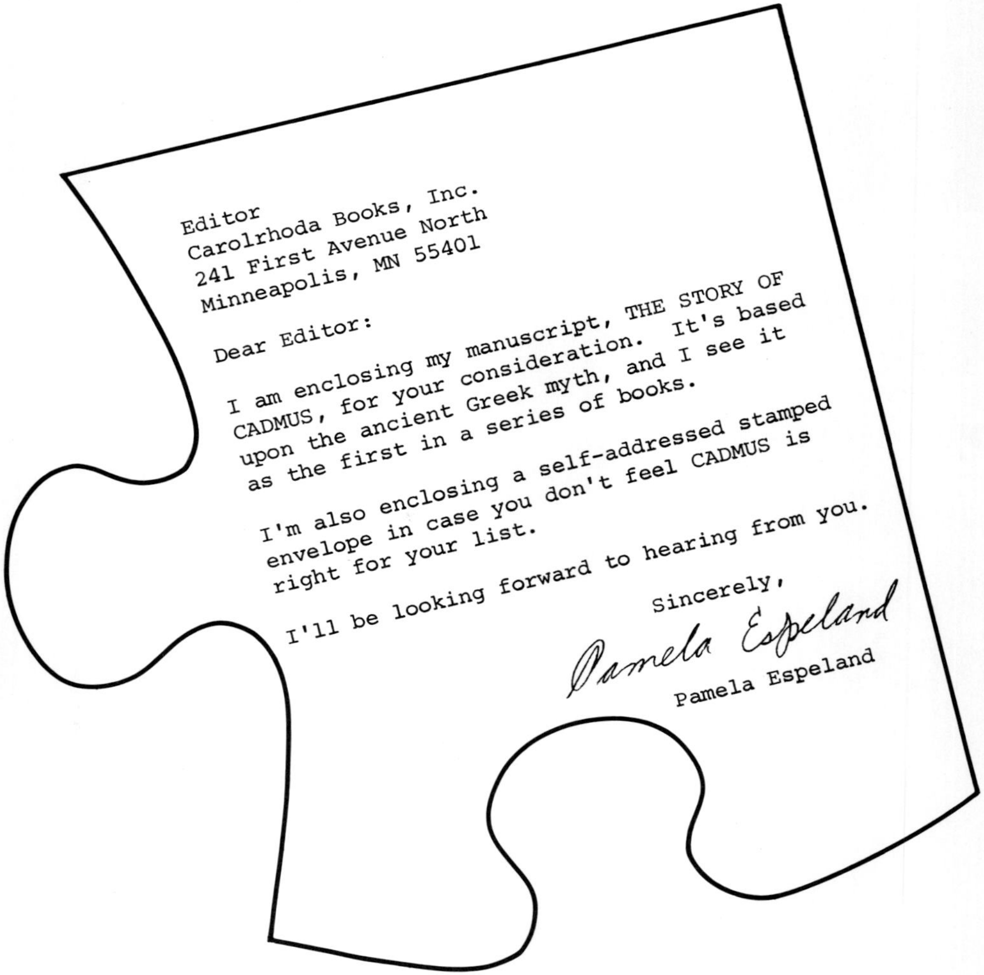

Editor
Carolrhoda Books, Inc.
241 First Avenue North
Minneapolis, MN 55401

Dear Editor:

I am enclosing my manuscript, THE STORY OF CADMUS, for your consideration. It's based upon the ancient Greek myth, and I see it as the first in a series of books.

I'm also enclosing a self-addressed stamped envelope in case you don't feel CADMUS is right for your list.

I'll be looking forward to hearing from you.

Sincerely,

Pamela Espeland

Pamela Espeland

The Puzzle of Books

by Michael Kehoe

Carolrhoda Books, Inc. Minneapolis

The author would like to thank everyone who contributed to the preparation of this book and who gave so generously of their time, expertise, and patience. A special thanks to Susan Pearson, Editor, Carolrhoda Books, Inc.; Richard (Dick) Hannah, Production Manager, Lerner Publications Co.; Pamela Espeland, Writer; Reg Sandland, Artist; Gale Houdek, Designer; Ken Pautzke, P & H Photo Composition; Gail Jensen, Typesetter; David Barnard, Keyliner; Richard Trombley, Cameraperson; Gary Hansen, Stripper; Harry Shafer and Dick Newman, Shafer & Feld, Inc.; Gary Erickson, Platemaker; Luke Pfleghaar, Printer; Jerry Hanson, Muscle Bound Bindery, Inc.

I would like to dedicate this book to my very good friend, my wife, Molly Greenman.

Publisher's Note: Every publisher works a little differently from every other, and the same holds true for typographers and printers. Add to that the different ways in which individuals work and the different machinery that can be used to do the same jobs, and you come up with any number of variations on the theme of how a book is made. THE PUZZLE OF BOOKS shows but one variation. For the sake of simplicity and clarity, the others have not been dealt with in this book.

LIBRARY OF CONGRESS CATALOGING IN PUBLICATION DATA

Kehoe, Michael.
The puzzle of books.

Summary: Follows the making of a book from writing and illustrating through editing, design, production, and binding, until it is shipped to a library or bookstore.
1. Books—Juvenile literature. 2. Printing, Practical—Juvenile literature. 3. Publishers and publishing—Juvenile literature. [1. Books. 2. Printing, Practical. 3. Publishers and publishing] I. Title.
Z4.Z9K4 070.5 81-17115
ISBN 0-87614-169-6 AACR2

3 4 5 6 7 8 9 10 90 89 88 87 86 85 84 83

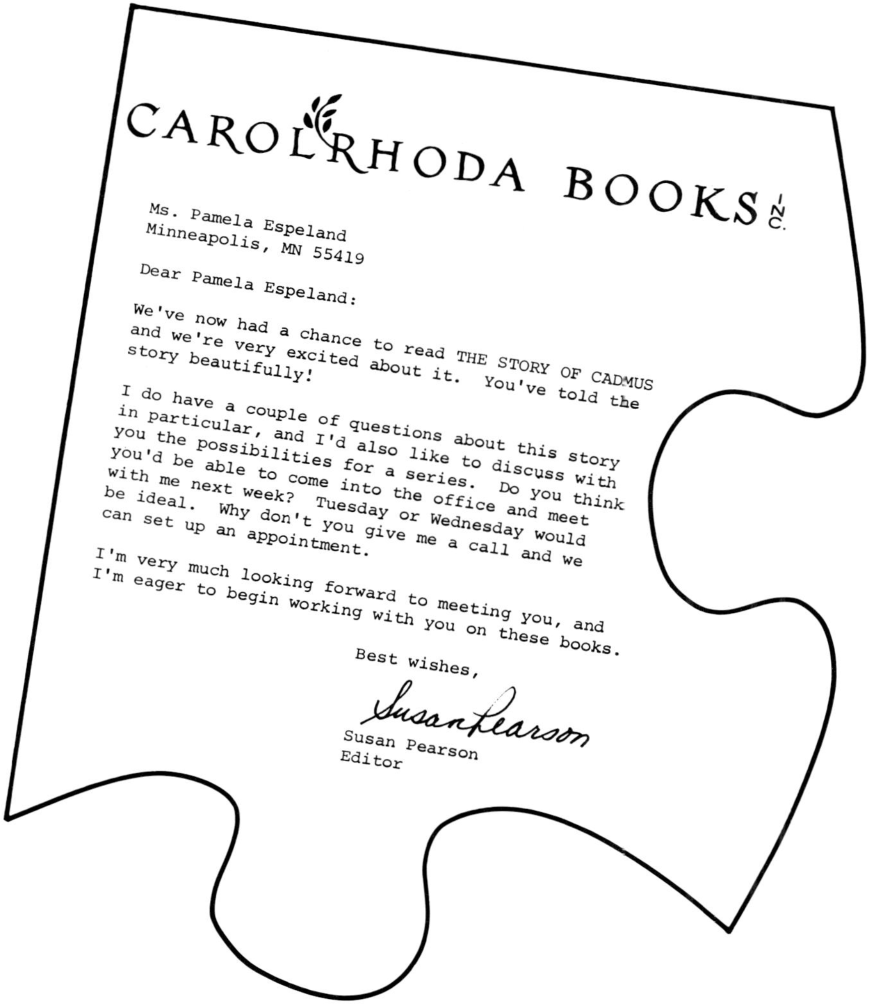

CAROLRHODA BOOKS INC.

Ms. Pamela Espeland
Minneapolis, MN 55419

Dear Pamela Espeland:

We've now had a chance to read THE STORY OF CADMUS and we're very excited about it. You've told the story beautifully!

I do have a couple of questions about this story in particular, and I'd also like to discuss with you the possibilities for a series. Do you think you'd be able to come into the office and meet with me next week? Tuesday or Wednesday would be ideal. Why don't you give me a call and we can set up an appointment.

I'm very much looking forward to meeting you, and I'm eager to begin working with you on these books.

Best wishes,

Susan Pearson

Susan Pearson
Editor

What a puzzle books are! Paper, pictures, type, cover—so many details it's a wonder that all the pieces fit together so neatly.

Just look at this page. It doesn't appear very complicated—just a few paragraphs of type on a plain white page. But many people were involved in making it. First someone had an idea and wrote it down. Others decided on the size of the page, the kind of paper to use, the style of type, and the width of the margins. Many more people were involved in printing the page and in binding the pages together. On the facing page are pictures of just a few of the people who helped to make this book.

The first piece of our book puzzle begins on the cover. The woman you see there is an author. She has begun to write a modern version of an ancient story called THE STORY OF CADMUS. In THE PUZZLE OF BOOKS, we will follow, from beginning to end, the making of CADMUS into a book.

When the author has finished writing the story, she types it neatly and sends it to a company called a publishing house or publisher. The story that she sends is called a manuscript. She asks the publisher to think about making her manuscript into a book.

Now the second piece of our puzzle enters the picture—the editor.

Editor

When a manuscript arrives in the mail at a publishing house, it is given to an editor to read. The editor must decide whether or not the story will make a good book. He or she must think about the people who have bought the other books the house has published. Will they buy this book too?

In the case of THE STORY OF CADMUS, the editor liked the manuscript and thought young readers would like it too. She decided to publish it.

From now on, this editor will be in charge of all the details involved in making THE STORY OF CADMUS into a book. She will watch over each piece of the puzzle to make sure it will fit with all the others.

The editor and author have a lot to talk about before the manuscript becomes a book.

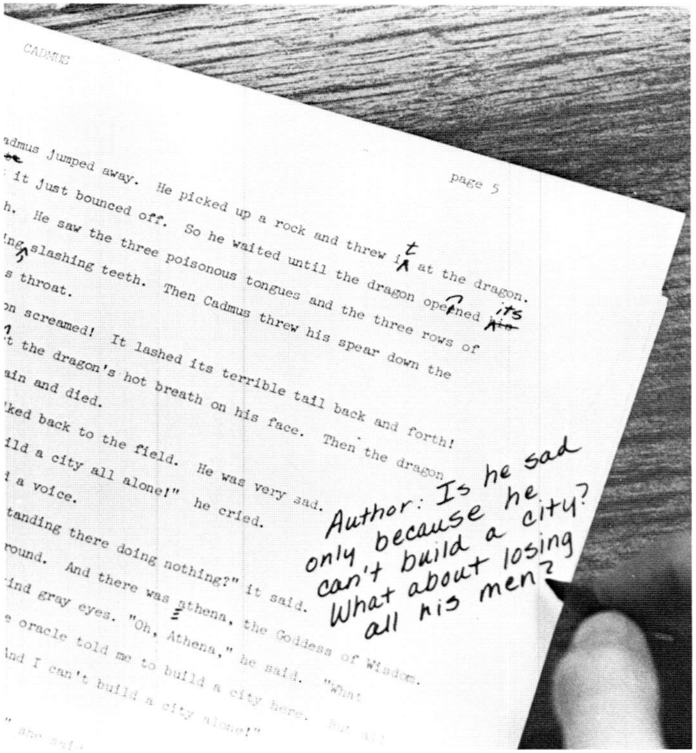

One of the editor's first responsibilities is to help the author make the story as clear as possible.

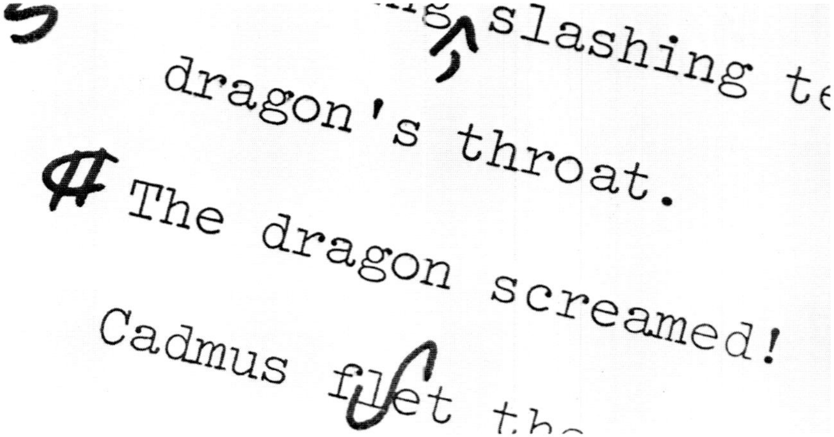

Sometimes commas have been left out of the manuscript, or new paragraphs need to be made, or words have been misspelled. The editor makes marks like these to correct the mistakes.

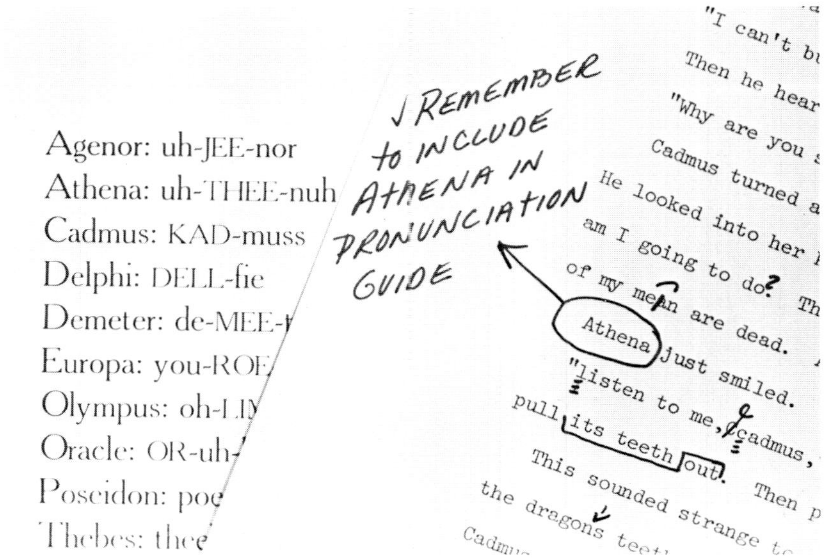

There are many strange words and names in THE STORY OF CADMUS, so the editor has suggested putting a pronunciation guide in the book.

Artist

While the editor was working on the manuscript, she was also thinking about pictures for it. By the time she has finished her work on the manuscript, she is ready to send it to an artist.

First the artist reads the story to see if he or she likes it and wants to illustrate it. If so, the artist will make some sample drawings to show the editor how he or she thinks the pictures should look.

After the editor has looked at the samples and discussed them with the author and with other people at the publishing house, she and the artist have many decisions to make. What size should the book be? for example. Or how colorful should the pictures be? When questions like these have been answered, the artist can begin to work on the illustrations.

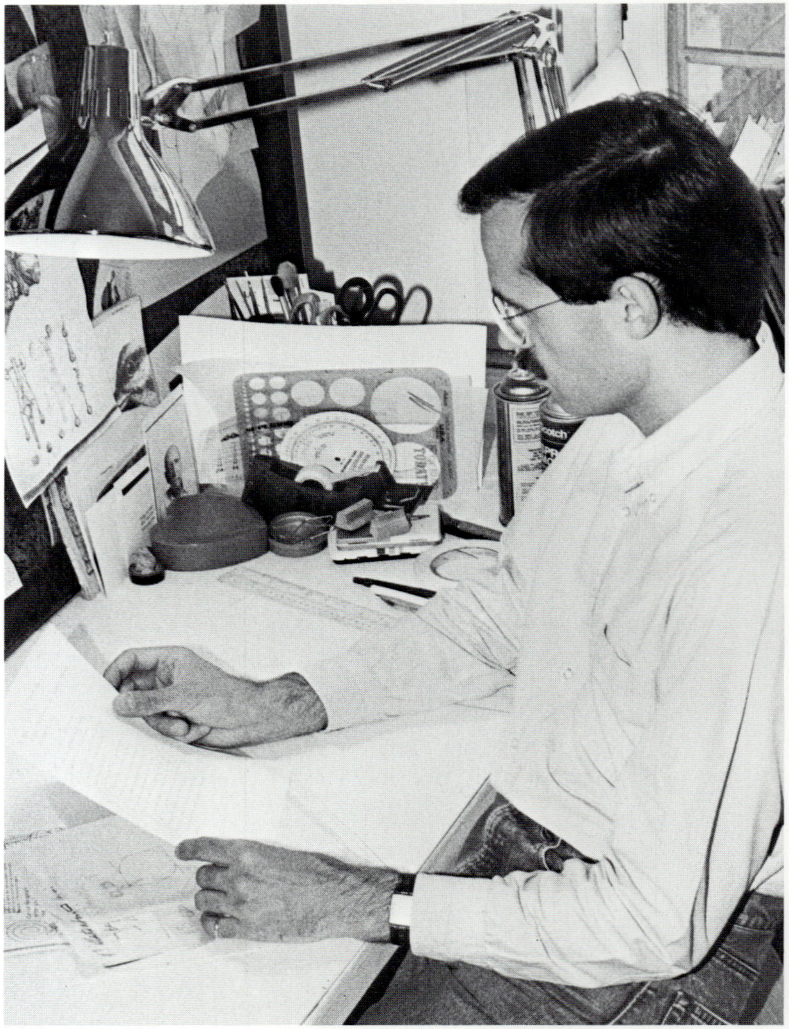

First the artist reads the story to see if he likes it and wants to illustrate it.

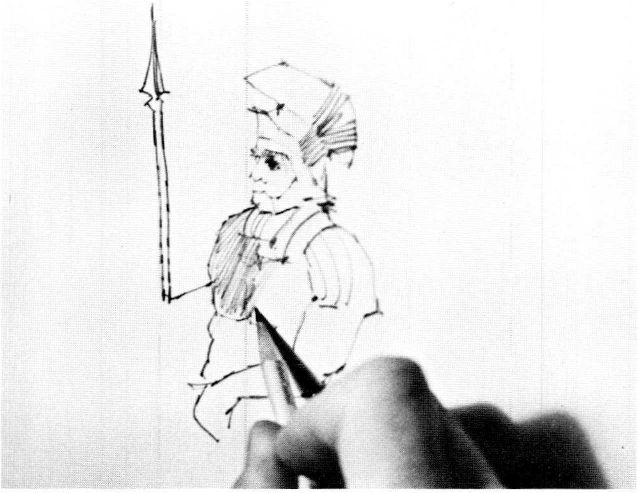

The artist is making a sketch to show the editor how he thinks the soldiers in the story should look.

Once the artist and the editor have agreed about how the pictures should look, what size the book should be, and other things, the artist is ready to make a book "dummy." The dummy is the artist's model of the book. It begins as a blank book the same size and shape as the finished book will be. The artist cuts the manuscript apart and pastes the story into the dummy where he wants it to go. He then makes sketches of all the illustrations and pastes them into the dummy too.

The dummy will give the editor a good idea of how the artist would like the final book to look. It also gives her a chance to suggest changes before the artist does the final drawings.

Designer

After the editor has carefully gone over the dummy, she meets with the production manager and the designer. The production manager looks closely at the sample drawings to make sure there won't be problems later when it is time to print the book.

The editor and designer talk about how the final book should look. What type should they use? Should it be simple or fancy? Should it be heavy or light? They also look at the papers they have to choose from.

After they have talked, the designer chooses a typeface and a paper. He or she decides how wide the margins should be. And the designer may have other ideas that will make the book more attractive. The designer and the editor will discuss all these ideas, and together they will make the final decisions.

The editor meets with the production manager and the designer.

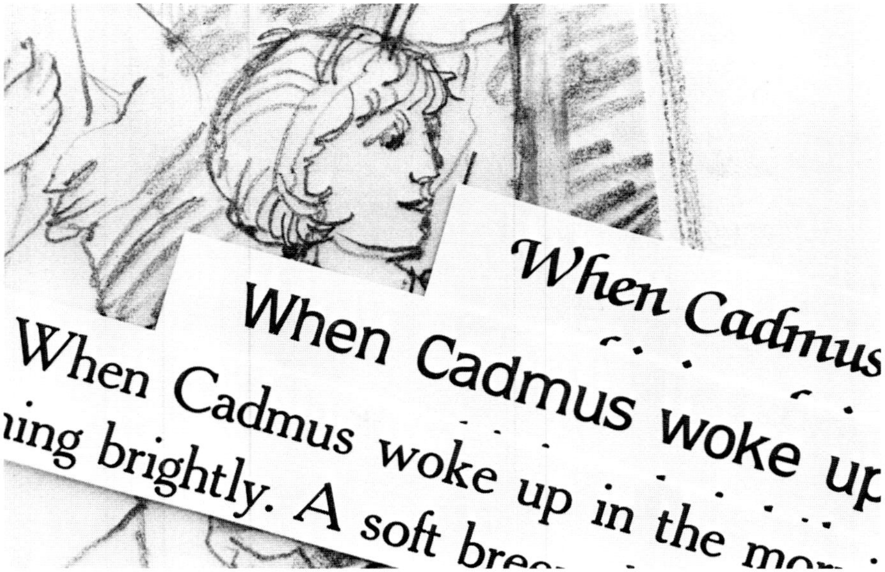

The designer has suggested using fancy capital letters for the first letters on some pages. To give the editor a clear idea of what she has in mind, she makes a tracing.

There are hundreds of different typefaces to choose from. The designer suggested three different styles that might be good for CADMUS. She and the editor agreed that the third one would be best.

There are many different kinds of paper to choose from too. Some are smooth; others are rougher. Some are pure white; others are creamy. The designer looks for one that will go well with the artwork.

Typesetter

After a typeface has been chosen, the entire manuscript must be set into type. This is done by a typesetter at a company called a typographer.

At one time typesetting was all done by hand. The typesetter would assemble each word in the story, one by one, using pieces of metal with one letter on each piece. This process was called "composing," and typographers are still often called compositors. Today most typesetting is done with the help of computers.

The typesetter works at a computer console which has a typewriter keyboard and a television-like screen.

The album on the left holds a blank disc. When the typesetter types THE STORY OF CADMUS on the keyboard, the blank disc records the letters in the form of magnetic codes. When the entire story has been recorded on this disc, it is run through the computer again and the letters are transferred onto a program disc.

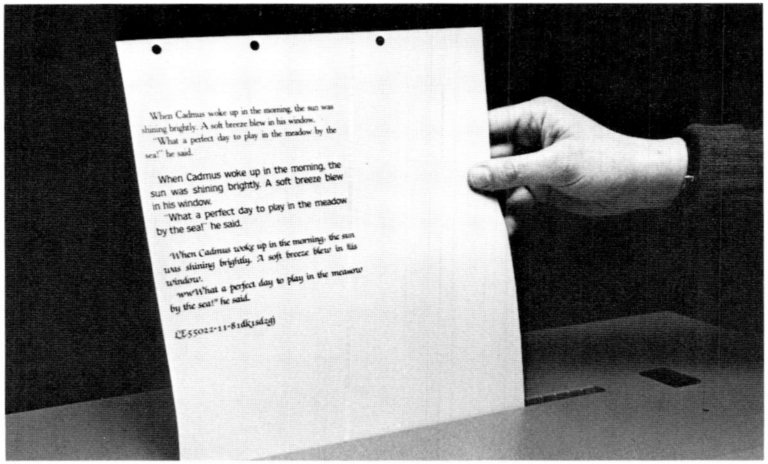

The program disc is then put into a printing machine along with a typestyle disc, which contains the alphabet in the typeface chosen by the editor and the designer. This printing machine combines the information from both discs and transfers it to photographic paper. But you cannot see the words on the paper yet. Like film, it must be developed first. When the paper has been developed, CADMUS will be printed on it.

Keyliner

At the same time that the type is being set, the artist is busy working on the illustrations. Finally the type is ready and the artist has delivered all his artwork to the editor.

Now it's time for the keyliner to go to work. The keyliner, also called a paste-up artist, will paste the type and photocopies of the illustrations onto paper boards in exactly the positions they are to have in the finished book. These boards will be photographed and the film will be used to make the book, so the keyliner must be very careful and measure everything exactly when he or she works. Otherwise when the book is printed, a line might be crooked, like this one!

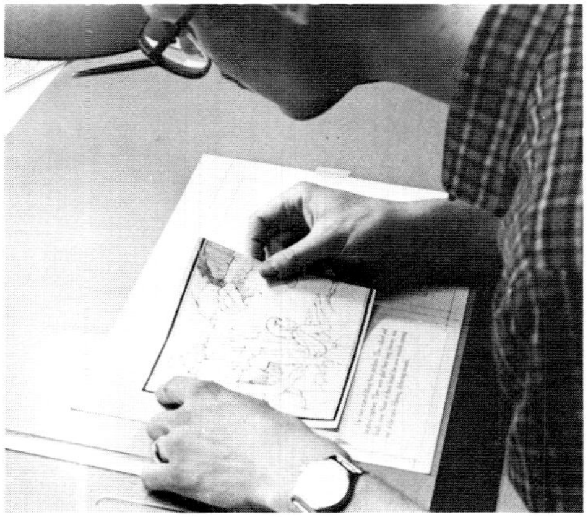

Each board will have two pages on it. When the book is finished, these two pages will face each other. First the keyliner draws guidelines on the boards. Then he pastes type and art onto the left-hand page.

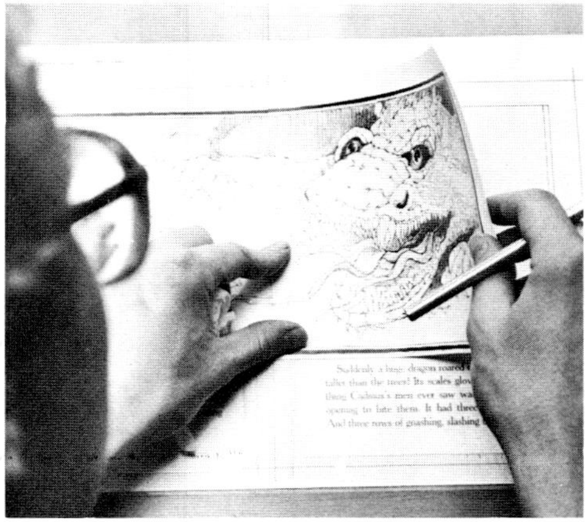

When he has finished with the left-hand page, the keyliner moves on to the right. The finished board with everything pasted on is called a keyline or a mechanical. There will be a keyline for every page in the book.

Cameraperson

When the keylines are finished, the editor checks them. If everything is all right, they then go on to the cameraperson.

The cameraperson photographs the text and the illustrations. He or she then processes the film and ends up with negatives. The negatives are transparent in the areas that were black on the keylines and black in the areas that were white.

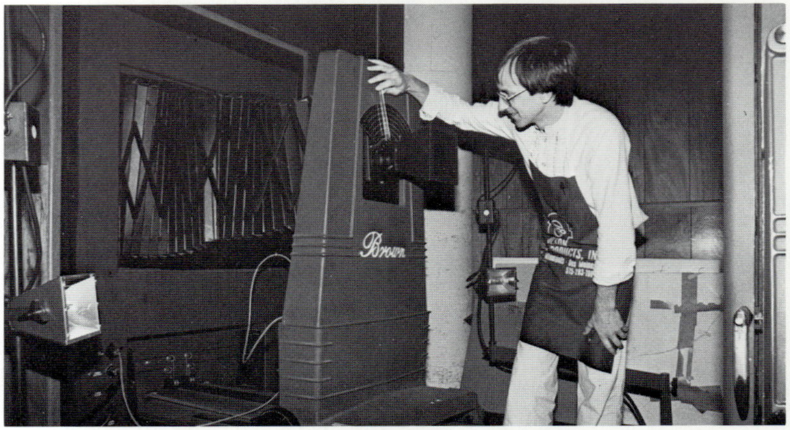

The cameraperson adjusts the lens of his huge camera.

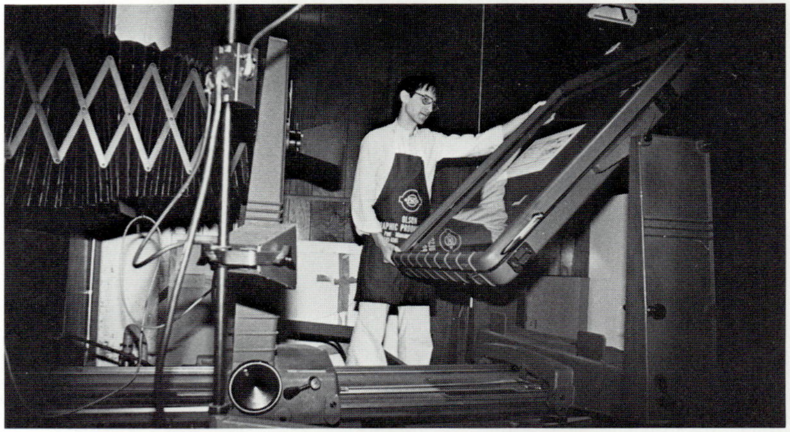

Then he swings the copyboard, onto which he has attached the keyline he is going to photograph, into position in front of the lens.

Now the cameraperson goes to the rear of the camera (in another room) to load it with film. Then he takes the picture. After the picture has been taken, the film is put through a film processing machine in order to develop it.

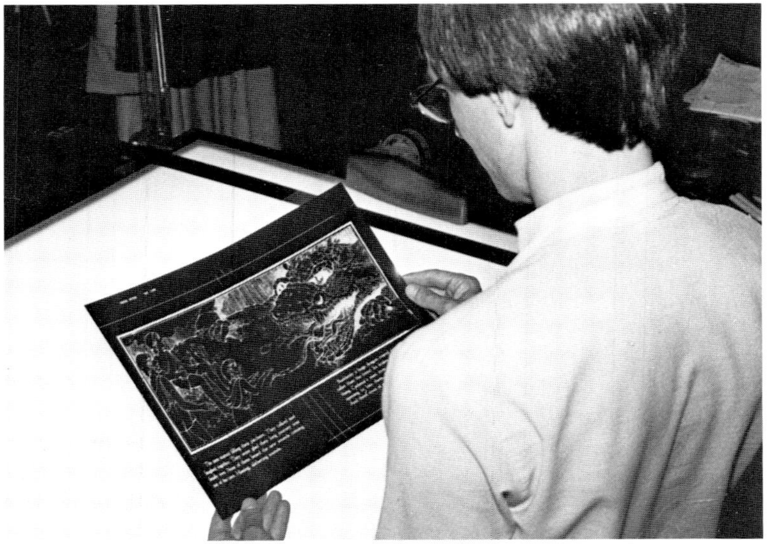

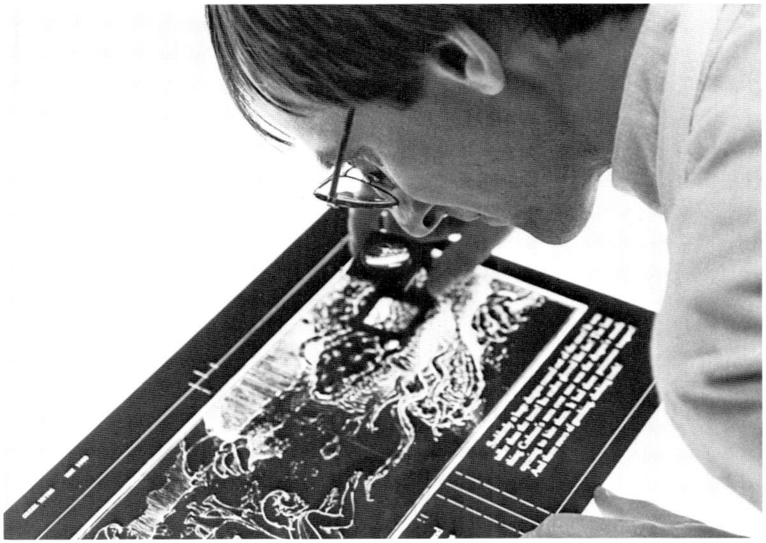

At last the cameraperson has a film negative. Now he must check it carefully to make certain every detail has come out clean and sharp. He uses a magnifying glass to help him.

Stripper

When the cameraperson has made negatives of the keylines, the negatives are given to the stripper. The stripper attaches them to large sheets of plastic. In the photograph on the right, you can see that some of the negatives are attached upside down, others are attached right-side up, and the pages don't seem to be in any order. Actually the way the negatives have been positioned on the sheet has been very carefully planned. When the stripper has finished one plastic sheet of negatives . . .

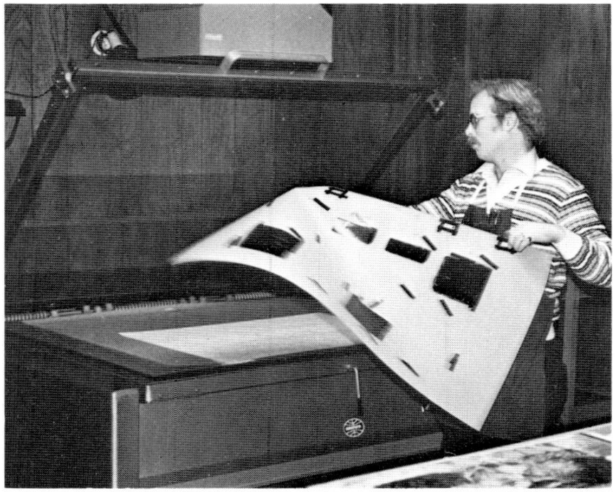

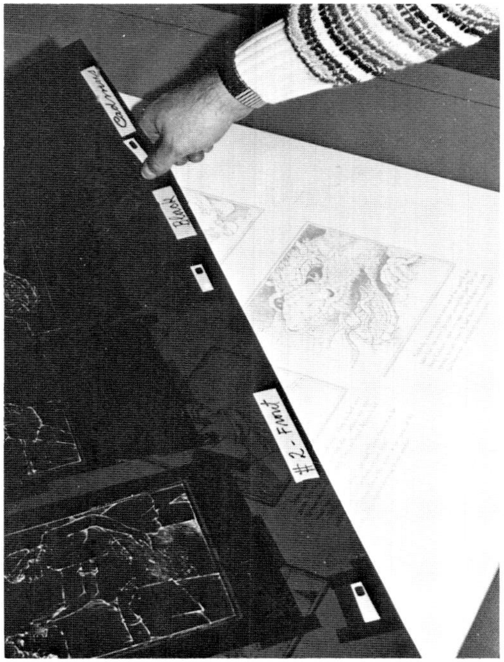

. . . he puts it into a machine along with one piece of chemically treated "proof" paper. Then he shines a strong light over them both. Where the film is transparent, the light will shine onto the paper and turn it dark. Where the film is black, the light will not go through and the paper will stay the same.

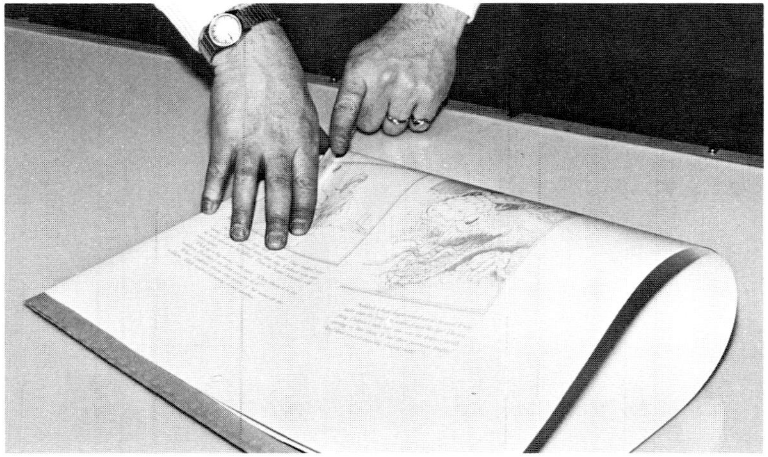

Other pictures and type will go on the reverse side of the proof paper. Then the stripper folds the proof paper, staples it, and trims off the edges. If everything has been done correctly, it will look like 16 pages of a real book when he opens it. Every page will be right-side up and in the right order. Both the stripper and the editor will check this proof very carefully.

Platemaker

The last step that must be taken before CADMUS can be printed is the making of printing plates. The process that the platemaker uses to make plates is similar to the process that the stripper used to make proofs. But instead of using sheets of proof paper, the platemaker uses sheets of aluminum.

When the type and art on the plastic sheets of negatives have been duplicated on sheets of aluminum, these sheets (called plates) can be used over and over again to print the pages of CADMUS.

The platemaker puts a plastic sheet of negatives into a machine along with a sheet of chemically treated aluminum. A strong light will make the type and pictures on the negative appear on the aluminum plate.

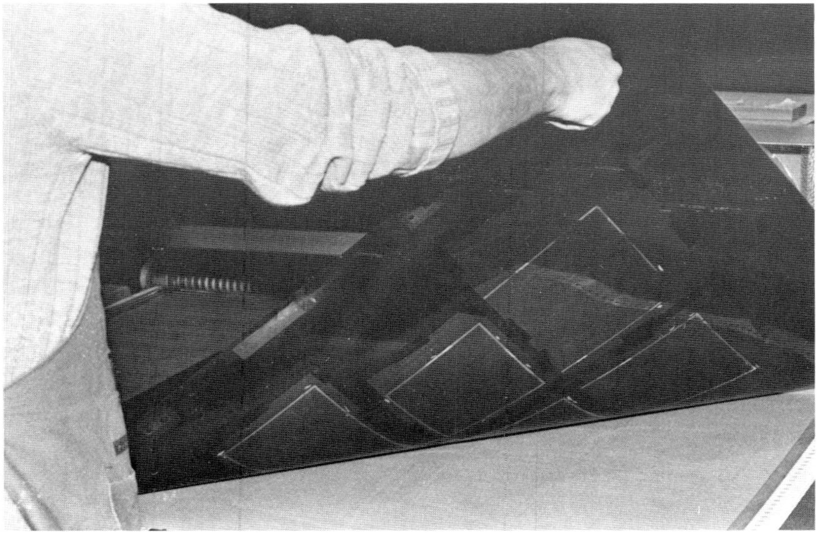

The images on the negatives are now on the aluminum plate. But you can't see them yet. First the plate must be developed. The platemaker lays the plate in the developing sink and pours developer over it.

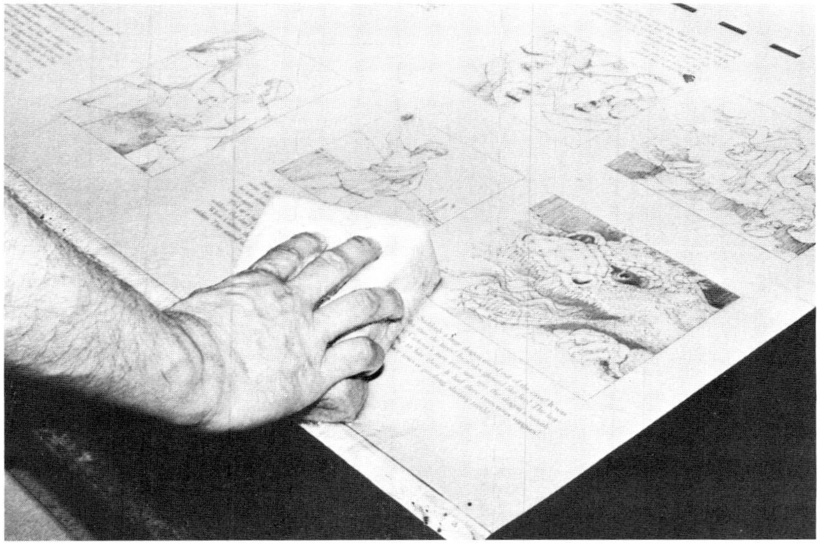

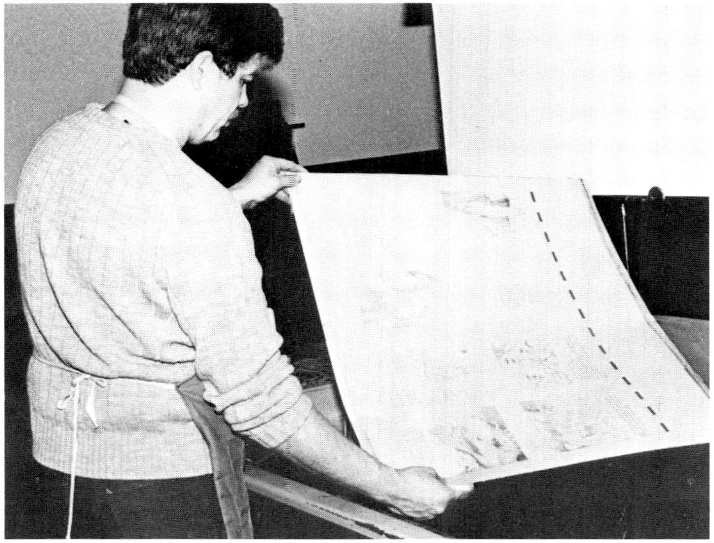

As the developer spreads over the plate, the images begin to show. When the images are clear, the platemaker washes the plate and dries it.

Printer

At last THE STORY OF CADMUS is ready to be printed! The pages of a book are printed by a machine called a printing press, and the people who operate the press are called printers. First one of the plates the platemaker has made is attached to the press. When the press is running, the part of the plate on which there is type and art will be covered with ink. As paper passes through the press, the ink on the plate will be transferred to the paper.

When all the paper has been printed on one side, the plate is removed and another plate is attached. The paper is turned over and run through the press again. Now both sides of one sheet have been printed.

The printer examines the printing press to make sure everything is in good working order for the printing of CADMUS.

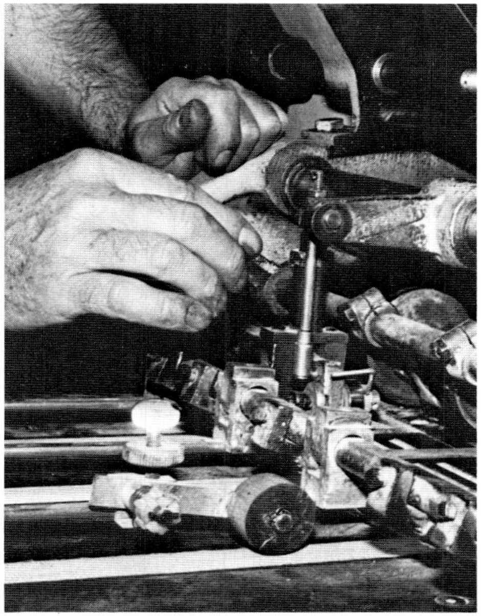

Blank sheets of paper are taken from storage and loaded into the press. The paper is stacked high. Then the mechanism that feeds the paper into the press is adjusted.

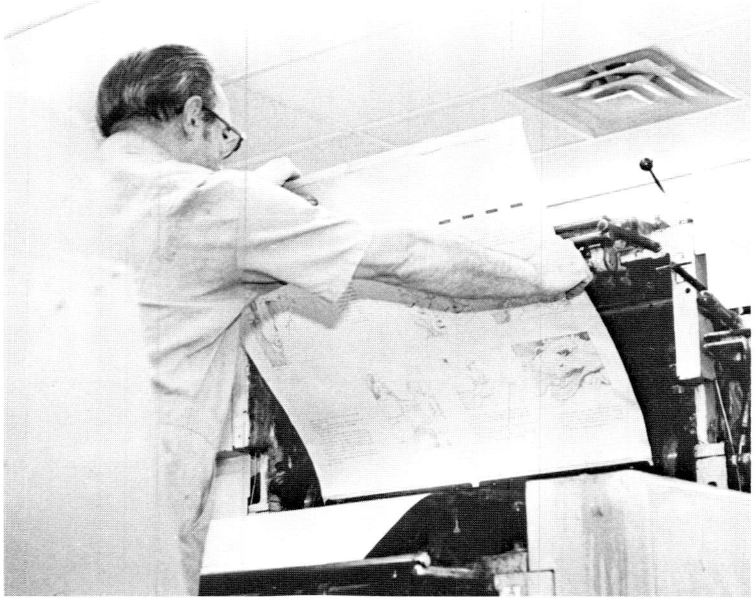

Now the printer attaches the printing plate to the press. The plate wraps around a cylinder called a drum. The printer uses a wrench to fasten it on.

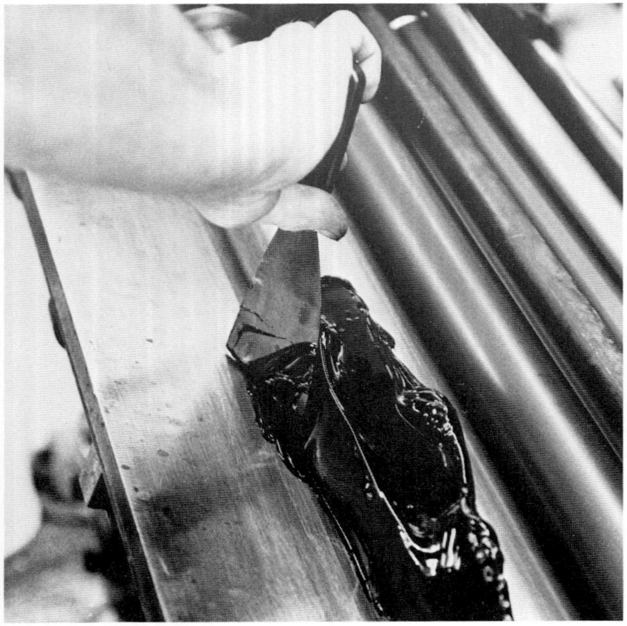

The printer carefully spreads ink along rollers which will transfer the ink onto the plate. Everything is now ready. Roll the press!

Slowly the drum and the plate begin to spin. Hundreds of moving parts clatter with a sound that the printer listens to like a doctor listens to your heart. When it sounds just right, he reaches for a knob and brings the press up to operating speed. When this press is running at full speed, it can print about 6,000 sheets in one hour.

Printed sheets begin to stack up. Quickly the printer pulls a sheet out of the press so it can be examined.

Together the printer and the production manager from the publishing house look over the printed sheet. They compare it to the original artwork to make sure everything looks the way it should. When all the sheets have been printed on both sides, they are stacked on a skid for shipment to a bindery.

Binder

THE STORY OF CADMUS is nearly finished. All that remains to be done is to bind the printed sheets together and put them between covers. These last steps all take place at a book bindery. At the bindery, many people use a number of machines to bind and cover the books. The steps they go through are:

A. FOLDING

B. GATHERING

C. SEWING

D. TRIMMING

E. MAKING COVERS

F. CASING-IN

Once these steps have been completed, the book will look just like the books found in a library, a bookstore, at school, or at home.

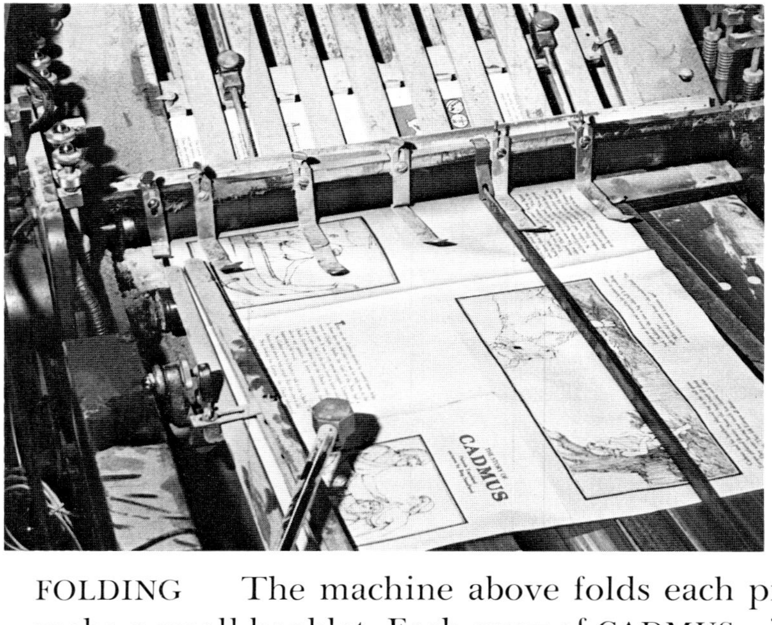

FOLDING The machine above folds each printed sheet, called a signature, several times to make a small booklet. Each copy of CADMUS will have two signatures.

GATHERING Next, the two signatures are loaded separately into another machine. This machine will take one signature from each stack and glue them together.

SEWING The combined signatures are now taken to a sewing machine which stitches them along the back. The method of sewing used by this bindery is side-sewing. A book that has been side-sewn is very strong.

TRIMMING Once the signatures have been sewn together, the edges must be trimmed off. Huge blades on the trimming machine cut the edges and make all the books exactly the same size.

MAKING COVERS While the insides of CADMUS were being worked on, a cover was also illustrated, designed, and printed on paper or cloth. Now the paper or cloth is glued onto cardboard pieces by yet another machine in order to make the book covers. Book covers are called cases.

CASING-IN When both the cases and the signatures have been completely assembled, a machine glues them together. Then dust jackets can be put on. The book is finished! It can now be wrapped with other copies of CADMUS and sent to a warehouse for storing and shipping.

After nearly a year of careful preparation, THE STORY OF CADMUS is at last a book. Schools, libraries, and bookstores all across the country have ordered it from the publisher and it has been shipped to them from the warehouse. And when you, the reader, check the book out of a library or buy it from a bookstore, then the last piece of our PUZZLE OF BOOKS will be in place.